Team Spirit

THE CHARLOTTE BOBCATS

BY

MARK STEWART

Content Consultant
Matt Zeysing
Historian and Archivist
The Naismith Memorial Basketball Hall of Fame

NORWOOD HOUSE PRESS

CHICAGO, ILLINOIS

Norwood House Press
P.O. Box 316598
Chicago, Illinois 60631

For information regarding Norwood House Press, please visit our website at:
www.norwoodhousepress.com or call 866-565-2900.

All photos courtesy of AP Images—AP/Wide World Photos, Inc. except the following:
Ned Dishman/NBAE/Getty Images (cover);
Topps, Inc. (14, 35 bottom left, 36, 40 top and bottom left, 43);
Author's Collection/Charlotte Bobcats (16); Ned Dishman/NBAE/Getty Images (cover).
Special thanks to Topps, Inc.

Editor: Mike Kennedy
Associate Editor: Brian Fitzgerald
Designer: Ron Jaffe
Project Management: Black Book Partners, LLC.
Special thanks to Gloria Miller

Library of Congress Cataloging-in-Publication Data

Stewart, Mark, 1960-
    The Charlotte Bobcats / by Mark Stewart ; content consultant,
Matt Zeysing.
        p. cm. -- (Team spirit)
    Summary: "Presents the history, accomplishments and key person-
alities of the Charlotte Bobcats basketball team. Includes timelines,
quotes, maps, glossary and websites"--Provided by publisher.
    Includes bibliographical references and index.
    ISBN-13: 978-1-59953-123-6 (lib. bdg. : alk. paper)
    ISBN-10: 1-59953-123-2 (lib. bdg. : alk. paper)
    1. Charlotte Bobcats (Basketball team)--History--Juvenile litera-
ture. I. Zeysing, Matt. II. Title.
GV885.52.C45S734 2008
796.323'640975676--dc22
                                                    2007013759

COVER PHOTO: Adam Morrison, Jake Voskuhl, and Jeff McInnis huddle to talk
during the 2006–07 season.

Table of Contents

SPORTS WORDS & VOCABULARY WORDS: In this book, you will find many words that are new to you. You may also see familiar words used in new ways. The glossary on page 46 gives the meanings of basketball words, as well as "everyday" words that have special basketball meanings. These words appear in **bold type** throughout the book. The glossary on page 47 gives the meanings of vocabulary words that are not related to basketball. They appear in ***bold italic type*** throughout the book.

BASKETBALL SEASONS: Because each basketball season begins late in one year and ends early in the next, seasons are not named after years. Instead, they are written out as two years separated by a dash, for example 1944–45 or 2005–06.

Meet the Bobcats

Most predators hunt animals that are smaller, weaker, or slower. A bobcat is different. Its prey is often larger, stronger, and faster. The same could be said of the Charlotte Bobcats. They are only a few seasons old, but they have already shown they can take down the best teams in the **National Basketball Association (NBA)**.

The Bobcats play hard and smart. They *savor* their victories and learn from their losses. The Bobcats compete with great energy and enthusiasm. They take the court each game believing they can win.

This book tells the story of the Bobcats. They are the top team in a state famous for its basketball history, yet their own story is just beginning. The fans have been watching with excitement as Charlotte tries to build a team ready to challenge for a championship. They root for the Bobcats with all their heart. Even when Charlotte faces bigger, stronger, or faster opponents, the team is always in the hunt.

Walter Herrmann and Jake Voskuhl hug during a game in March 2007. Charlotte fans love to cheer for their hardworking team.

Way Back When

The Bobcats came to be on December 18th, 2002. On that day, the NBA decided to expand from 29 teams to 30. The Bobcats filled an opening left by a team called the Hornets. They had played in Charlotte, North Carolina for 14 seasons before moving to New Orleans, Louisiana. A wealthy businessman named Robert L. Johnson wanted to bring basketball back to Charlotte. The NBA gave him the go-ahead, and a few weeks later he began building his club. Their first season would be 2004–05.

North Carolina was a perfect choice for the NBA. Basketball has been a popular sport in the state for ***generations***. Duke University, North Carolina State University, and the University of North Carolina are among the nation's best college teams every year. Each of these schools has won the **National Championship. Professional** basketball has also had a proud history in North Carolina. Before the Hornets made Charlotte their home in the 1980s, the Carolina Cougars were one of the top teams in the **American Basketball Association (ABA)** in the 1970s.

North Carolina was also known for producing some of the sport's greatest players, including Lou Hudson, Bob McAdoo, Dominique Wilkins, James Worthy, David Thompson, and Michael Jordan. Jordan would later join the Bobcats as the head of basketball operations.

The team's first players came from a special **expansion draft**. The other NBA teams were allowed to protect eight players on their **roster**, and the Bobcats then chose from all those who were left unprotected. Among the players that Charlotte selected were center Primoz Brezec and forwards Jason Kapono and Gerald Wallace. All three had played in the NBA, but each had watched from the bench while backing up starting players.

Next, the Bobcats participated in the **NBA draft**. They picked second and chose Emeka Okafor, a powerful center who had shared **College Player of the Year** honors in 2004. Over the next few months, the Bobcats also signed two experienced guards, Brevin Knight and Steve Smith. They would give the young team good leadership.

LEFT: Robert L. Johnson, the man who started the Bobcats.
ABOVE: Michael Jordan during his days at the University of North Carolina.

On November 4th, 2004, the Bobcats played their first NBA game. A huge crowd of 23,319 fans jammed into the Charlotte Coliseum to watch them face the Washington Wizards. The starting **lineup** was Brezec, Okafor, Wallace, Knight, and Kapono. Brezec scored the team's first basket. The Wizards won, but the fans went home happy. NBA basketball had returned to Charlotte.

The Bobcats won 18 games and lost 64 in their first season. There were exciting victories, heartbreaking defeats, and many wonderful performances. Okafor was the team's star. He led the Bobcats in minutes, points, rebounds, and blocked shots. During one stretch, Okafor reached double-figures in points and rebounds in 19 games in a row. It was the longest streak by an NBA **rookie** in 35 years!

LEFT: Emeka Okafor, a shining star of the Bobcats. **ABOVE**: The crowd stands to watch the opening tip-off of the team's first game.

The Team Today

As with any new team, the Bobcats took a while to start believing in themselves. Many times during their first two seasons, they led games heading into the fourth quarter only to lose in the final 12 minutes. Slowly but surely, the Bobcats gained the confidence they needed. In 2005–06, they improved to 26 victories.

The master plan for the Bobcats began to take shape during the 2006–07 season. Their young stars were becoming comfortable on the court. Their older players were earning the respect they had sought while playing for other teams.

With a core of talented and experienced players, the Bobcats are ready to take the next step. The team will continue to search for **free agents** and consider different trades to strengthen its roster. The Bobcats do not just look for good players. They want good people. The Bobcats believe that they need players who combine great talent with a winning attitude to become a championship team.

Young stars Raymond Felton and Adam Morrison were both top draft picks for the Bobcats.

Home Court

The Bobcats played their first season at Charlotte Coliseum and then moved to Charlotte Bobcats Arena. Their current home is a great place to watch a game. Most fans enter the arena through a four-story *atrium*. They often stop to look at a large *mosaic* that shows the history of basketball in North Carolina.

The seats in Charlotte's arena may be the only ones in the league that an NBA player could actually fit in. They are wide and comfortable, with plenty of legroom. In a special area called Rock the Rooftop, Bobcats fans can do some indoor **tailgating**.

The centerpiece of the Bobcats' home is its gigantic scoreboard. At 36 feet wide and 38 feet high, it features the largest scoreboard video screen in the country. Sitting atop the scoreboard is a *three-dimensional* model of the Charlotte skyline.

BY THE NUMBERS

- *There are 19,026 seats for basketball in Charlotte Bobcats Arena.*
- *The first game in the arena was held on November 5th, 2005. The Bobcats beat the Boston Celtics in **overtime** 107–105.*
- *The scoreboard in the arena weighs 40 tons.*

The scoreboard at Charlotte Bobcats Arena is one of the coolest in the NBA.

Dressed for Success

Charlotte's team colors are Bobcats Orange, Bobcats Blue, and white. They also use gray, silver, and black on their uniforms. The Bobcats usually wear white at home and either orange or blue when they play on the road. Their home uniforms have the team name across the chest. Their main road uniform has the city name across the chest.

The Bobcats have two **logos**. Both feature a snarling bobcat. The one the team uses on its shorts shows the bobcat in front of a basketball. Charlotte's logo is different from those of most other NBA teams because its mascot is seen from the side.

Bobcats are the top predators in many parts of North Carolina. The team chose its name after fans submitted more than 1,000 entries in a naming contest. Some believe that the team's owner, Robert L. Johnson, liked the name because he is a "cat named Bob."

Jake Voskuhl models the team's home uniform.

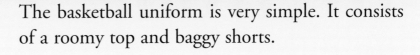

The basketball uniform is very simple. It consists of a roomy top and baggy shorts.

- The top hangs from the shoulders, with big "scoops" for the arms and neck. This style has not changed much over the years.

- Shorts, however, have changed a lot. They used to be very short, so players could move their legs freely. In the last 20 years, shorts have gotten longer and much baggier.

Basketball uniforms look the same as they did long ago … until you look very closely. In the old days, the shorts had belts and buckles. The tops were made of a thick cotton called "jersey," which got very heavy when players sweated. Later, uniforms were made of shiny *satin*. They may have looked great, but they did not "breathe." As a result, players got very hot! Today, most uniforms are made of *synthetic* materials that soak up sweat and keep the body cool.

Gerald Wallace slams one down in Charlotte's road uniform. The team also wears blue uniforms for away games.

We Won!

2004-05 CHARLOTTE BOBCATS INAUGURAL SEASON YEARBOOK

BOBCATS

Charlotte big on Bobcats

Bobcats go with Bickerstaff

BOBCATS SCORE OKAFOR

CHARLOTTE BOBCATS

The first victory for a new sports team is an important occasion. For some teams, it comes early in the season. For others, the wait for win number one can be *agonizingly* long. The Bobcats got their first "W" in just their second game.

Charlotte coach Bernie Bickerstaff thought the Bobcats might win their season opener, against the Washington Wizards. The team had the lead in a close game, but the Wizards pulled ahead in the final minutes for a 103–96 victory. The Bobcats were determined not to let their next chance slip away.

Charlotte hosted the Orlando Magic a few nights later. The Bobcats and Magic battled back and forth for the first 15 minutes of the game. Then, late in the second quarter, the Charlotte defense clamped down and held Orlando scoreless for more than four minutes. At halftime, the Bobcats were ahead 49–42.

The second half was amazing. The Bobcats came roaring out of the locker room. They outscored the Magic by 13 points to start the third quarter. When guard Jason Hart threw an **alley-oop pass** and Gerald Wallace slammed the ball into the basket, Charlotte Coliseum exploded in cheers. The Bobcats now led 64–44.

Coach Bickerstaff had seen a lot of NBA games and knew that a 20-point lead could disappear quickly. He remembered the loss to the Wizards and how his team was gasping for air by the end of the game. Bickerstaff pleaded with his players to pace themselves. Guards Brevin Knight and Steve Smith set an example for their teammates. Smith scored several

LEFT: Thousands of fans who saw the Bobcats' first victory left the arena with this souvenir yearbook.   **ABOVE**: Jason Hart drives to the hoop against the Magic.

important baskets, and Knight provided calm and confident leadership.

The most interesting battle on the court was between the teams' two young centers, Emeka Okafor of the Bobcats and Dwight Howard of the Magic. Howard had been the top pick in the draft a few months earlier. Okafor was taken right after him with the second pick. In the game, Okafor got the best of Howard with 12 points and 14 rebounds.

With Knight, Smith, and Okafor leading the way, the Bobcats won 111–100. After the team returned to the locker room, Hart— who had played the best game of his NBA career—presented the game ball to team owner Robert L. Johnson. The shouts, smiles, and laughter made Bickerstaff proud.

"These young men deserve this," the coach said. "They played hard. We made plays when we had to make plays."

LEFT: Emeka Okafor pulls a rebound away from Dwight Howard in the first of their many NBA meetings.
ABOVE: Bernie Bickerstaff is delighted with his team's effort.

Go-To Guys

To be a true star in the NBA, you need more than a great shot. You have to be a "go-to guy"—someone teammates trust to make the winning play when the seconds are ticking away in a big game. Bobcats fans have had a lot to cheer about over the years, including these great stars …

THE PLAYERS

PRIMOZ BREZEC — 7' 1" Center

- BORN: 10/2/1979
- FIRST SEASON WITH TEAM: 2004–05

Primoz Brezec was the first player selected by the Bobcats in the 2004 expansion draft. Though he had been in the NBA for three years, he had spent most of those seasons sitting on the bench of the Indiana Pacers. The Bobcats knew Brezec was a good shooter and rebounder. He just needed more playing time to improve his defense. Brezec scored the first basket in the history of the Bobcats.

LEFT: Primoz Brezec
TOP RIGHT: Emeka Okafor
BOTTOM RIGHT: Brevin Knight

EMEKA OKAFOR 6' 10" Forward/Center

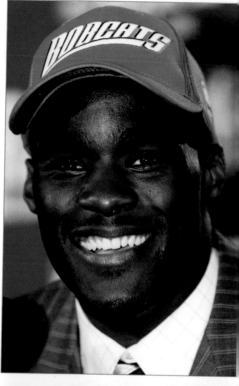

- BORN: 9/28/1982
- FIRST SEASON WITH TEAM: 2004–05

Emeka Okafor led his college squad to the National Championship in 2004. The Bobcats thought he was the perfect player to build their team around and chose him with the second pick in the NBA draft. Okafor made Charlotte look smart. In his first season, he was named NBA **Rookie of the Year**.

BREVIN KNIGHT   5' 10" Guard

- BORN: 11/8/1975
- FIRST SEASON WITH TEAM: 2004–05

The Bobcats needed an experienced point guard to lead their young team, and Brevin Knight was the right man for the job. He made good passes, controlled the pace of the game, played great defense, and almost never turned the ball over to the opposing team. Knight's knowledge of the sport helped his teammates become better players.

GERALD WALLACE   6' 7" Forward

- BORN: 7/23/1982
- FIRST SEASON WITH TEAM: 2004–05

When the Bobcats picked Gerald Wallace off the roster of the Sacramento Kings, they believed he was a quick-thinking guard in a high-flying forward's body. They were correct. Wallace turned out to be an excellent defensive player who stole passes and blocked shots as well as anyone in the NBA. Wallace also proved he could score. The fans nicknamed him "G-Force."

RAYMOND FELTON   6' 1" Guard

- BORN: 6/26/1984
- FIRST SEASON WITH TEAM: 2005–06

Raymond Felton looked like he was born to play point guard. Fans of the University of North Carolina thought so, especially after he guided the Tar Heels to the 2005 NCAA Championship. When Felton came to the Bobcats, he set his sights on winning an NBA title for Charlotte. In his first year, he showed he was ready to take charge. Felton led the team in minutes played and was one of the top scorers among all NBA rookies.

SEAN MAY   6' 9"   Forward

- BORN: 4/4/1984
- FIRST SEASON WITH TEAM: 2005–06

Basketball is the family business in the May home. Sean May's father, Scott, was the college Player of the Year in 1976, when his team won the National Championship. The younger May starred in the 2005 **NCAA Tournament**, when he won a National Championship of his own. A big, strong forward, May scored with a gentle shooting touch.

ADAM MORRISON   6' 8"   Forward

- BORN: 7/19/1984
- FIRST SEASON WITH TEAM: 2006–07

In his first NBA season, Adam Morrison showed that he was one of the game's most competitive players. He was willing to do whatever it took to score and was not afraid to go nose-to-nose with the league's best defenders. Morrison was the top scorer in college in 2006. With the Bobcats, he proved that he could put the ball in the basket from anywhere on the court.

TOP LEFT: Gerald Wallace
BOTTOM LEFT: Raymond Felton
TOP RIGHT: Sean May   **BOTTOM RIGHT**: Adam Morrison

On the Sidelines

The Bobcats have had some amazing people working behind the scenes for them. Their owner, Robert L. Johnson, was the first African-American to become a *majority owner* of a major sports team. Johnson started Black Entertainment Television (BET) in the 1980s. In 2001, he sold the company for $3 billion. From the time he bought the Bobcats, Johnson insisted that his players get involved with the community. He has donated millions of dollars to local youth programs.

Charlotte's first coach was Bernie Bickerstaff. He was chosen because he was a good teacher as well as a good coach. Bickerstaff previously coached in Seattle, Washington, and Denver, and was named NBA **Coach of the Year** in 1986–87. He helped the Bobcats learn what it takes to win in the NBA.

Michael Jordan was the man hired to make basketball decisions for the Bobcats. Jordan grew up in North Carolina and played college basketball there, so his job with Charlotte was a kind of "homecoming." Jordan was put in charge of sizing up talent and sharing his championship attitude with his players.

Michael Jordan joined the Bobcats in 2006. He was chosen to help the team develop a winning attitude.

One Great Day

When Charlotte fans got the schedule for the 2004–05 season, their eyes were drawn immediately to the games against the Detroit Pistons. The Pistons had just won the NBA Championship. It had been more than 30 years since an **expansion team** had beaten the defending league champion. The Bobcats would have four chances to match this feat.

In their first meeting of the season, the Bobcats and Pistons played a thrilling game that took two overtimes to decide. Detroit won 117–116. A few days later, they met again, in Charlotte. Having come so close the first time, the Bobcats were confident they could defeat the Pistons. The fans were not as certain. The Bobcats had lost seven games in a row.

The Bobcats held their own against the Pistons in the first quarter. In the second quarter, Detroit built a small lead, but Charlotte caught fire and outscored the Pistons by 19 points over the next nine minutes. Emeka Okafor pumped in six points in the last 90 seconds of the first half to give the Bobcats a 51–35 lead.

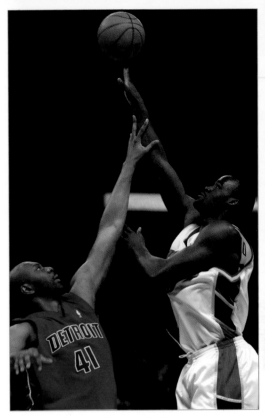

Emeka Okafor is fouled as he shoots over Elden Campbell of the Pistons.

Could Charlotte maintain its **momentum** in the second half? Okafor answered that question by scoring 10 of his team's first 14 points in the third quarter. As the final period began, the Bobcats were ahead by a score of 73–54.

In their earlier meeting, the Pistons had erased a 13-point lead by the Bobcats. This time, they came back again. With less than two minutes left, Charlotte was up by only six points. Okafor came to the rescue again with a layup that allowed the Bobcats and their fans to breathe a little easier. Charlotte held on to win 91–89. Okafor finished with 22 points and 15 rebounds.

"That was one we needed to get through," coach Bernie Bickerstaff said with relief. "You could see it on our faces that we might have been waiting for something bad to happen. The bottom line is that you have to play to win."

"It felt good," added Okafor. "Everybody was really focused. We came determined to get this one. When we have taken big leads, we have lost it like that so many times. We came back strong and pulled out a victory."

Legend Has It

Did Primoz Brezec once fall off a cliff?

LEGEND HAS IT that he did. As a 12-year-old boy in Slovenia, Brezec was fooling around on his bike and accidentally pedaled off a cliff near his family's home. He fractured his spine in the fall and spent five months in a body cast. Luckily, he made a full recovery.

Who was the best tackler on the Bobcats?

LEGEND HAS IT that John Outlaw was. No, tackling is not allowed in basketball. Outlaw, an **assistant coach** with the Bobcats, did his hard hitting in the **National Football League (NFL)**. He played for 11 seasons with the New England Patriots and Philadelphia Eagles. Outlaw then coached a college football team for 11 years. He got his first job in basketball from Bernie Bickerstaff. They began working together in 1990, with the Denver Nuggets.

Gerald "G-Force" Wallace blocks a shot by LeBron James of the Cleveland Cavaliers.

Which Bobcat set an NBA defensive record in 2006?

LEGEND HAS IT that Gerald Wallace did. During the 2005–06 season, Wallace had 135 steals and 113 blocks in 56 games. He became the first forward to average more than two steals and two blocks per game in the same season. The only other players to do this were both centers—Hakeem Olajuwon and David Robinson.

It Really Happened

When an NBA team puts a lot of young players in its lineup, you never know what to expect. No one, however, thought history would be made when the Bobcats met the Indiana Pacers on New Year's Eve 2006.

Adam Morrison was on fire in the first half. He scored 17 points against Indiana's tough defense. The Bobcats led 54–50 at halftime. The two teams played an exciting third quarter, as Charlotte clung to the lead.

When the Pacers pulled ahead early in the fourth quarter, the Bobcats kept their cool. Normally, Brevin Knight took charge of the team's offense at these times. However, he was injured and could not play. Raymond

Felton replaced him and set up one basket after another with his smart passing.

When the final buzzer sounded, the Bobcats had won 113–102. Morrison's long **3-pointer** with three minutes left ended Indiana's chances. The first-year forward finished with 30 points. Felton, in only his second season, had 19 **assists**.

After the game, the Bobcats went to the record books and were amazed by what they found. Only once before in the NBA had a player under the age of 23 scored more than 30 points in a game while an under-23 teammate handed out more than 15 assists.

Michael Jordan, who was watching from the stands, knew who the first two players were. He and Enis Whatley had done it in 1985 when they were rookies with the Chicago Bulls.

LEFT: Raymond Felton looks for an open teammate.
ABOVE: Adam Morrison goes up for a basket against the Pacers.

Team Spirit

Going to a Bobcats game is an unforgettable experience. There is a lot of color, action, and energy in the team's arena. The fun starts as fans walk into the building. Echoing through the **concourse** is the beat of the Rhythm Cats, a group of drummers that performs before and during games. They share the court with the Lady Cats dance team and Rufus Lynx, the team's mascot. His name in the opposite order—*lynx rufus*—is the scientific name for a bobcat.

When the Bobcats built their arena, they asked the designers to create most of the seats as if they were "courtside." This makes it easier for fans to get involved in the games. As the Charlotte players sprint up and down the court, they can *feel* the crowd cheering for them. It is almost as though the fans are right on the bench.

The fans at the Bobcats games often include celebrities from the world of auto racing and the sport of golf. Movie stars and singers are also frequent visitors to Charlotte games. In fact, the rapper Nelly is a part-owner of the team.

NASCAR star Jeff Gordon smiles during a Bobcats game. He is one of many celebrities who enjoys a night out at the team's arena.

Timeline

The basketball season is played from October through June. That means each season takes place at the end of one year and halfway through the next. In this timeline, the accomplishments of the Bobcats are shown by season.

2001–02
The Hornets play their final season in Charlotte.

2003–04
The team hires Bernie Bickerstaff as coach.

2002–03
The NBA approves an expansion team in Charlotte.

The Bobcats and Hornets do battle. The Hornets called Charlotte "home" before the Bobcats arrived.

The Bobcats' famous scoreboard shows a picture of the new arena.

2004–05
The Bobcats finish 18–64 in their first season.

2006–07
Matt Carroll leads the Bobcats in 3-point baskets.

2005–06
The Bobcats move into their new arena.

Emeka Okafor, Charlotte's "blue chip" star.

Matt Carroll fires a long jump shot.

Fun Facts

MISSION ACCOMPLISHED

When Gerald Wallace heard there would be a new team in Charlotte, he ordered his **agent** to get him on it. "I told him a year before the Bobcats picked their team that I had to be on that team," Wallace remembers. "If he didn't get me on it, he was fired!"

DEALING WITH IT

Adam Morrison eats a steak and baked potato two hours and 15 minutes before each game. He has Type I *diabetes* and needs to digest a big meal before he plays. Morrison also must monitor his blood sugar during games.

OLD SCHOOL

Matt Carroll, who joined the Bobcats in their first season, has a famous grandfather. Don Graham won more games than any high-school basketball coach in Pennsylvania history.

HAIR TODAY

The 2006–07 Bobcats had two players who were instantly recognized around the NBA for their hairstyles. Adam Morrison's mop-top and Walter Herrmann's long, golden locks made both players stand out wherever they went.

FLIGHT PLAN

When the team was deciding on a name, Bobcats was one of three final choices. The other two were Dragons and Flight. North Carolina was where the Wright Brothers flew the first airplane in 1903.

CAN I BUY A VOWEL?

In 2005, Emeka Okafor competed on the television show *Wheel of Fortune*. The money he won went to help the victims of Hurricane Katrina—many of whom were evacuated to Okafor's hometown of Houston, Texas.

LEFT: Gerald Wallace
ABOVE: Adam Morrison grabs a "hair-raising" rebound.

Talking Hoops

"We have a great young nucleus of players … the table is set."
—*Michael Jordan, on the future of the Bobcats*

"Right now I am just worrying about doing my job and doing it as well as I can, and nothing else."
—*Emeka Okafor, on staying focused in the NBA*

"I enjoy getting assists. I told these guys that's how I make my living, getting assists. So I'll just keep trying to do it."
—*Brevin Knight, on the thrill of making a good pass*

ABOVE: Michael Jordan
RIGHT: Raymond Felton and Bernie Bickerstaff

"It's the overall progress of the team I'm concerned with, and I think they've been doing a terrific job."
—*Bernie Bickerstaff, on the improvement shown by the Bobcats*

"Being known as a defensive player and for being aggressive is a really good thing for me because anybody can go out and score 30 points."
—*Gerald Wallace, on the importance of playing tough defense*

"We're starting to learn how to finish games now."
—*Raymond Felton, on the difference between winning and losing in the NBA*

For the Record

The great Bobcats players have left their marks on the record books. These are the "best of the best" …

Adam Morrison

BOBCATS AWARD WINNERS

WINNER	AWARD	SEASON
Emeka Okafor	NBA Rookie of the Year	2004–05
Emeka Okafor	NBA All-Rookie Team	2004–05
Raymond Felton	NBA All-Rookie Team	2005–06
Adam Morrison	NBA All-Rookie Team	2006–07

BELOW: Emeka Okafor shows his Rookie of the Year award.
RIGHT: Raymond Felton, a member of the 2006 NBA All-Rookie Team, is congratulated by his teammates.

Raymond Felton

Pinpoints

The history of a basketball team is made up of many smaller stories. These stories take place all over the map—not just in the city a team calls "home." Match the pushpins on these maps to the Team Facts and you will begin to see the story of the Bobcats unfold!

TEAM FACTS

1   Charlotte, North Carolina—*The Bobcats have played here since 2004.*

2   Benham, Kentucky—*Bernie Bickerstaff was born here.*

3   Marion, South Carolina—*Raymond Felton was born here.*

4   Sylacauga, Alabama—*Gerald Wallace was born here.*

5   Hickory, Mississippi—*Robert L. Johnson was born here.*

6   Chicago, Illinois—*Sean May was born here.*

7   Livingston, New Jersey—*Brevin Knight was born here.*

8   Brooklyn, New York—*Michael Jordan was born here.*

9   Glendive, Montana—*Adam Morrison was born here.*

10   Houston, Texas—*Emeka Okafor was born here.*

11   Santa Fe, Argentina—*Walter Herrmann was born here.*

12   Postojna, Slovenia—*Primoz Brezec was born here.*

Primoz Brezec

Play Ball

Basketball is a sport played by two teams of five players. NBA games have four 12-minute quarters—48 minutes in all—and the team that scores the most points when time has run out is the winner. Most baskets count for two points. Players who make shots from beyond the 3-point line receive an extra point. Baskets made from the free-throw line count for one point. Free throws are penalty shots awarded to a team, usually after an opponent has committed a foul. A foul is called when one player makes hard contact with another.

Players can move around all they want, but the player with the ball cannot. He must bounce the ball with one hand or the other (but never both) in order to go from one part of the court to another. As long as he keeps "dribbling," he can keep moving.

In the NBA, teams must attempt a shot within 24 seconds, so there is little time to waste. The job of the defense is to make it as difficult as possible for the offense to take a good shot—and to grab the ball if the other team shoots and misses.

This may sound simple, but anyone who has played the game knows that basketball can be very complicated. Every player on the court has a job to do. Different players have different strengths and weaknesses. The coach must mix these players in just the right way and teach them to work together as one.

The more you play and watch basketball, the more "little things" you are likely to notice. The next time you watch a game, look for these plays:

PLAY LIST

ALLEY-OOP—A play in which the passer throws the ball just to the side of the rim—so a teammate can catch it and dunk in one motion.

BACK-DOOR PLAY—A play in which the passer waits for a teammate to fake the defender away from the basket—then throws him the ball when he cuts back toward the basket.

KICK-OUT—A play in which the ball handler waits for the defense to surround him—then quickly passes to a teammate who is open for an outside shot. The ball is not really kicked in this play; the term comes from the action of pinball machines.

NO-LOOK PASS—A play in which a passer fools the defense by looking in one direction, then making a surprise pass to a teammate in another direction.

PICK-AND-ROLL—A play in which one player blocks, or "picks off," a teammate's defender with his body, then in the confusion cuts to the basket for a pass.

Glossary

BASKETBALL WORDS TO KNOW

3-POINTER—A basket made from behind the 3-point line.

AGENT—A person who represents a player in business matters.

ALLEY-OOP PASS—A ball thrown to a teammate as he begins to jump that enables him to dunk before he comes down.

AMERICAN BASKETBALL ASSOCIATION (ABA)—The basketball league that played for nine seasons starting in 1967. Prior to the 1976–77 season, four ABA teams joined the NBA, and the rest went out of business.

ASSISTANT COACH—A person who helps a team's head coach.

ASSISTS—Passes that lead to successful shots.

COACH OF THE YEAR—The award given each season to the league's best coach.

COLLEGE PLAYER OF THE YEAR—The award given each season to the nation's best college basketball player.

EXPANSION DRAFT—A meeting at which teams new to a league get to select players from teams already in the league.

EXPANSION TEAM—A new team that joins a league already in business.

FREE AGENTS—Players who are allowed to sign with any team that wants them.

LINEUP—The list of players who are playing in a game.

NATIONAL BASKETBALL ASSOCIATION (NBA)—The professional league that has been operating since 1946–47.

NATIONAL CHAMPIONSHIP—The title that college basketball teams play for at the end of each season.

NATIONAL FOOTBALL LEAGUE (NFL)—The league that started in 1920 and is still operating today.

NBA DRAFT—The annual meeting where teams pick from a group of the best college players.

NCAA TOURNAMENT—The competition that determines the champion of college basketball.

OVERTIME—The extra period played when a game is tied after 48 minutes.

PROFESSIONAL—Describes a player or team that plays a sport for money. College players are not paid, so they are considered "amateurs."

ROOKIE—A player in his first season.

ROOKIE OF THE YEAR—The annual award given to the league's best first-year player.

ROSTER—The list of players on a team.

TAILGATING—Parties held before and after a game, often in the parking lot outside the arena.

OTHER WORDS TO KNOW

AGONIZINGLY—In a way that causes great pain or stress.

ATRIUM—A large and airy central hall.

CONCOURSE—A long passageway.

DIABETES—A disease that affects a person's metabolism.

GENERATIONS—Periods of years roughly equal to the time it takes for a person to be born, grow up, and have children.

LOGOS—Symbols or designs that represents a company or team.

MAJORITY OWNER—The person among a group of owners who owns more than half of a company.

MOMENTUM—Strength or force built up during movement.

MOSAIC—A picture formed by assembling small pieces of tile or glass.

SATIN—A smooth, shiny fabric.

SAVOR—Enjoy fully and completely.

SYNTHETIC—Made in a laboratory, not in nature.

THREE-DIMENSIONAL—Appearing to have length, width, and depth.

Places to Go

ON THE ROAD

CHARLOTTE BOBCATS
333 East Trade Street
Charlotte, North Carolina 28202
(704) 688-8600

NAISMITH MEMORIAL BASKETBALL HALL OF FAME
1000 West Columbus Avenue
Springfield, Massachusetts 01105
(877) 4HOOPLA

ON THE WEB

THE NATIONAL BASKETBALL ASSOCIATION   www.nba.com
  • *Learn more about the league's teams, players, and history*

THE CHARLOTTE BOBCATS   www.bobcats.com
  • *Learn more about the Charlotte Bobcats*

THE BASKETBALL HALL OF FAME   www.hoophall.com
  • *Learn more about history's greatest players*

ON THE BOOKSHELF

To learn more about the sport of basketball, look for these books at your library or bookstore:

  • Thomas, Keltie. *How Basketball Works*. Berkeley, CA: Maple Tree Press, distributed through Publishers Group West, 2005.

  • Hareas, John. *Basketball*. New York, NY: Dorling Kindersley, 2005.

  • Hughes, Morgan. *Basketball*. Vero Beach, FL: Rourke Publishing, 2005.

47

Index

The Team

MARK STEWART has written more than 20 books on basketball, and over 100 sports books for kids. He grew up in New York City during the 1960s rooting for the Knicks and Nets, and now takes his two daughters, Mariah and Rachel, to watch them play. Mark comes from a family of writers. His grandfather was Sunday Editor of *The New York Times* and his mother was Articles Editor of *The Ladies' Home Journal* and *McCall's*. Mark has profiled hundreds of athletes over the last 20 years. He has also written several books about his native New York, and New Jersey, his home today. Mark is a graduate of Duke University, with a degree in History. He lives with his daughters and wife Sarah overlooking Sandy Hook, New Jersey.

MATT ZEYSING is the resident historian at the Basketball Hall of Fame in Springfield, Massachusetts. His research interests include the origins of the game of basketball, the development of professional basketball in the first half of the 20th century, and the culture and meaning of basketball in American society.